MW01477977

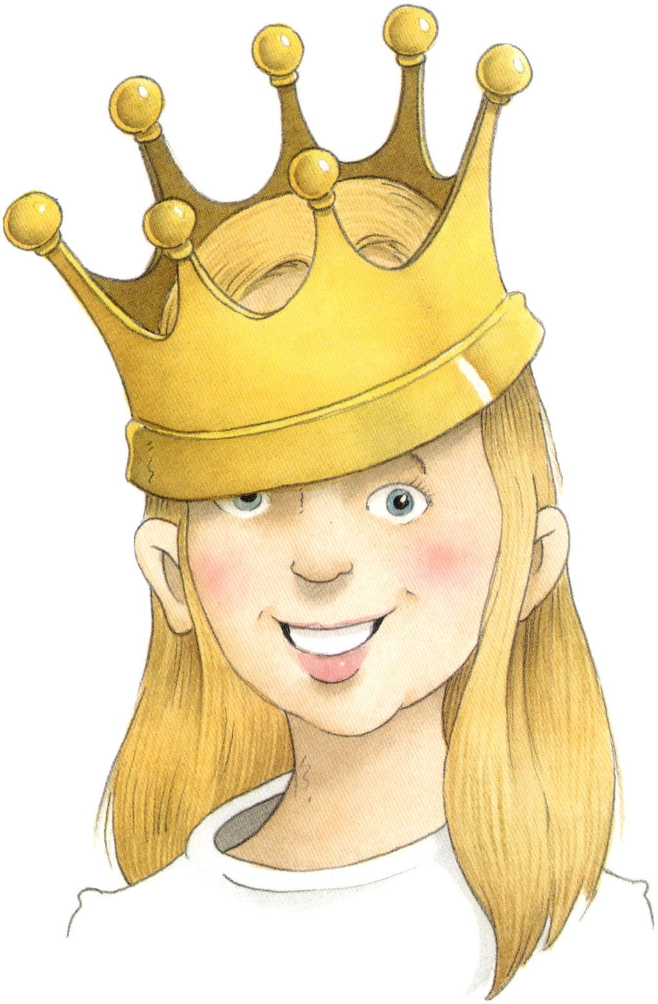

I AM

Story by
Etta Kaner

Pictures by
Steve Beinicke

A GROUNDWOOD BOOK
Douglas & McIntyre
Toronto/Vancouver

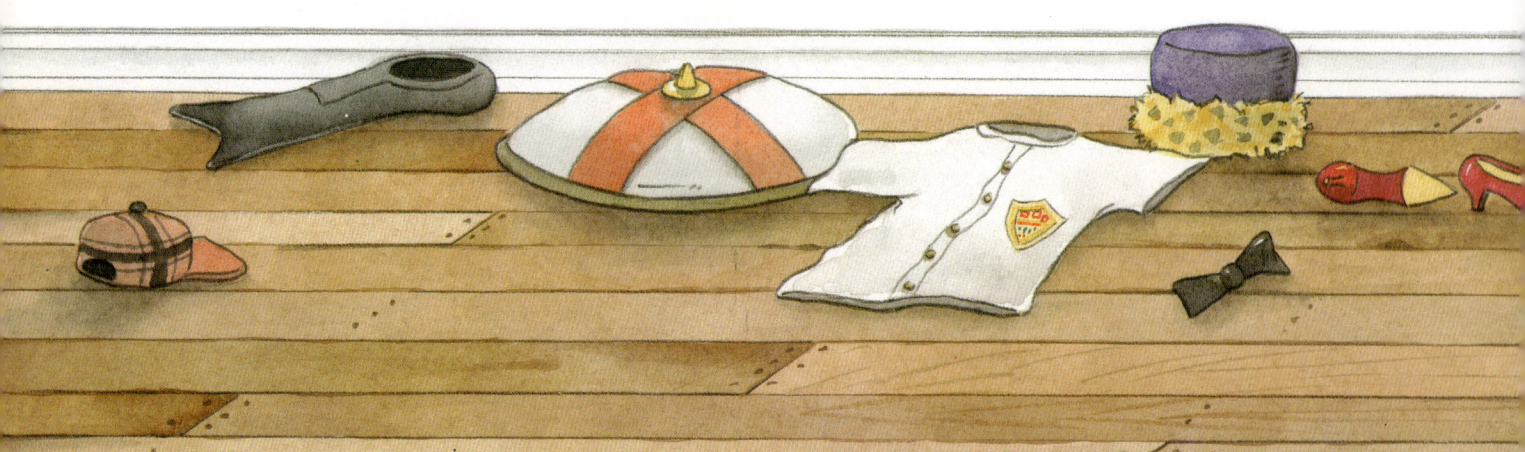

NOT JENNY

Text Copyright © 1991 by Etta Kaner
Illustrations Copyright © 1991 Steve Beinicke

All rights reserved. No part of this book may be reproduced or transmitted in any form or by any means without permission in writing from the publisher, except by a reviewer, who may quote brief passages in a review.

Groundwood Books/Douglas & McIntyre Ltd.
585 Bloor Street West
Toronto, Ontario   M6G 1K5

Canadian Cataloguing in Publication Data

Kaner, Etta
    I'm not Jenny

ISBN 0-88899-142-8

I. Beinicke, Steven, 1956–   II. Title.

PS8571.A64715 1991   jC813'.54   C91-093793-1
PZ7.K36Im 1991

Designed by Michael Solomon
Printed and bound in Hong Kong

For my parents,
Meilech and Sally Kaner
E.K.

To Jennifer, a real live girl
S.B.

Yesterday, when my sister sat down at the breakfast table, my mother said, "Good morning, Jenny."

"I am *not* Jenny," she announced. "I am a royal princess and I need a royal breakfast."

My mother scratched her head.
Instantly, there appeared in front of Jenny a silver bowl heaped with cereal, buttered toast on a jewelled plate, two boiled eggs with small crowns on top and a golden goblet filled with milk.

Jenny calmly ate her breakfast and got ready for school.

On the way to school, we met Jenny's friend Lisa.

"Hi, Jenny," said Lisa.

"She's not Jenny," I said. "She's a royal princess."

"I am *not* a royal princess," Jenny announced. "I am a brave knight and I'm on my way to fight a fierce dragon."

Lisa scratched her head.

Instantly, there appeared on the sidewalk an enormous fire-breathing dragon. His breath was so hot that it singed the grass and trees for seventeen blocks around.

Jenny pulled out her sword and drove it into the dragon's chest. He disappeared.

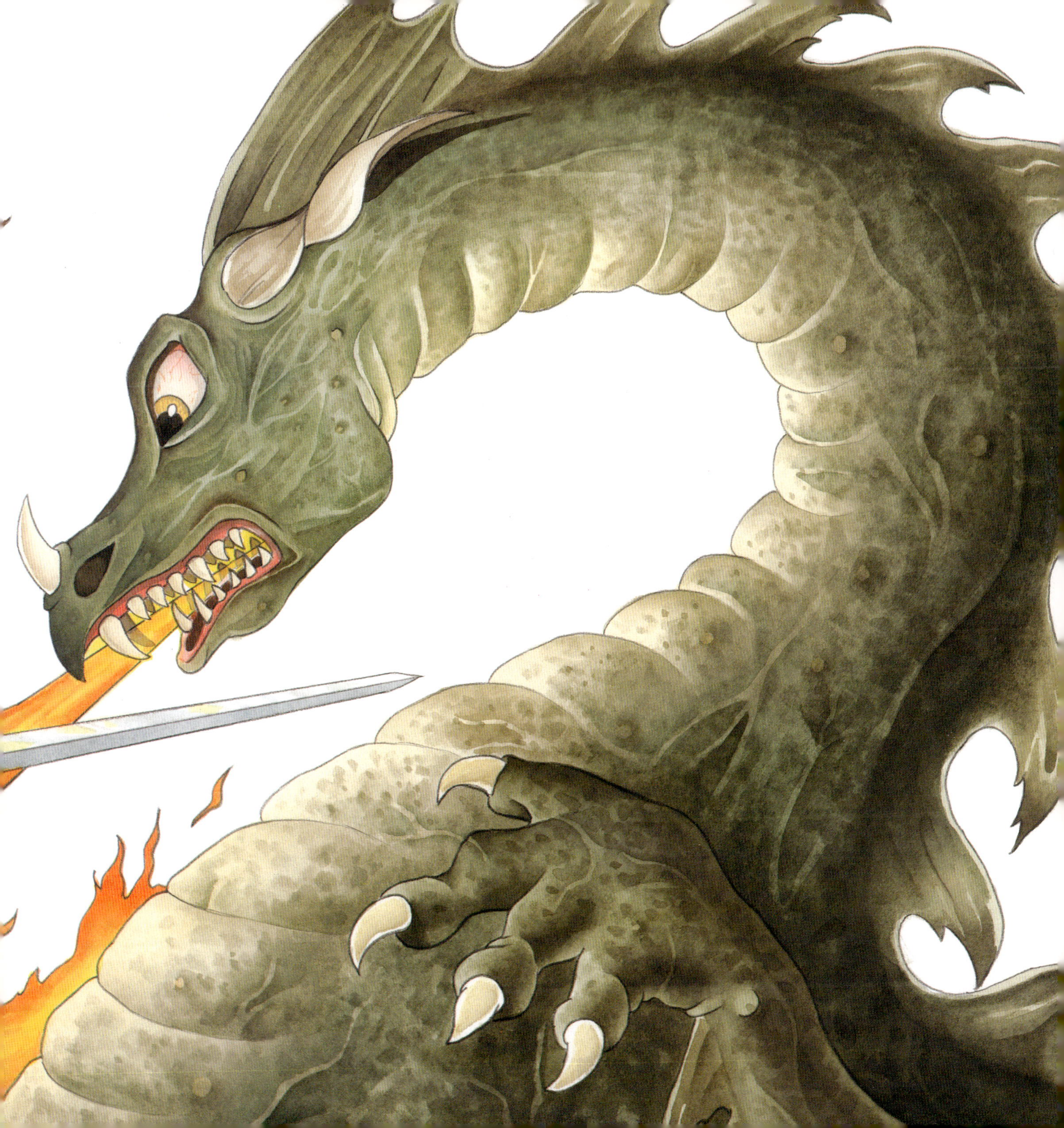

We passed by the seafood restaurant. We saw Mr. Berger unlocking his front door. Jenny waved to him.

"Hi, Jenny," he called.

"She's not Jenny," I said. "She's a brave knight who's just fought a fierce dragon."

"I am *not* a brave knight," said Jenny. "I am a deep sea diver and I take pictures of sea creatures."

Mr. Berger scratched his head.

Instantly, Jenny dove into Mr. Berger's giant fish tank. She swam around snapping pictures of the fish and lobsters inside the tank.

Jenny emerged from the water with a smile on her face. "Boy, did I ever get some great shots," she shouted.

I banged on the glass and yelled that we would be late for school.

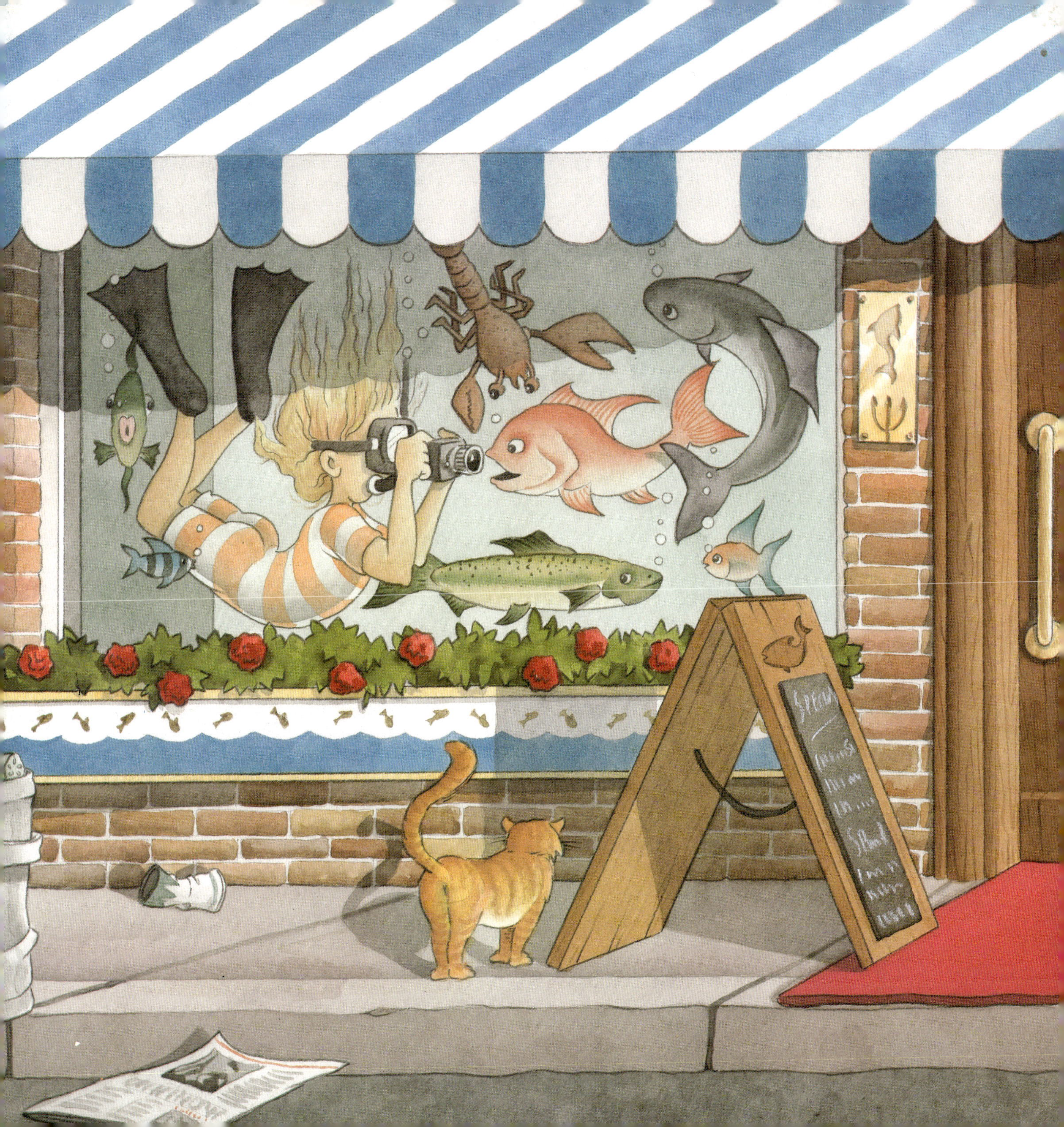

We ran the rest of the way to school. The teacher on duty exclaimed, "Goodness, how did you get so wet, Jenny?"

"She's not Jenny," I said. "She's a deep sea diver."

"I am *not* a deep sea diver," said Jenny. "I am a helicopter pilot."

The teacher scratched his head.

Instantly, a noisy helicopter with its blades whirring appeared in the schoolyard.

Jenny stepped into the pilot's seat, closed the door, and the helicopter took off into the air.

It flew over the school, over the treetops and into the distance. I was afraid that I'd never see Jenny again.

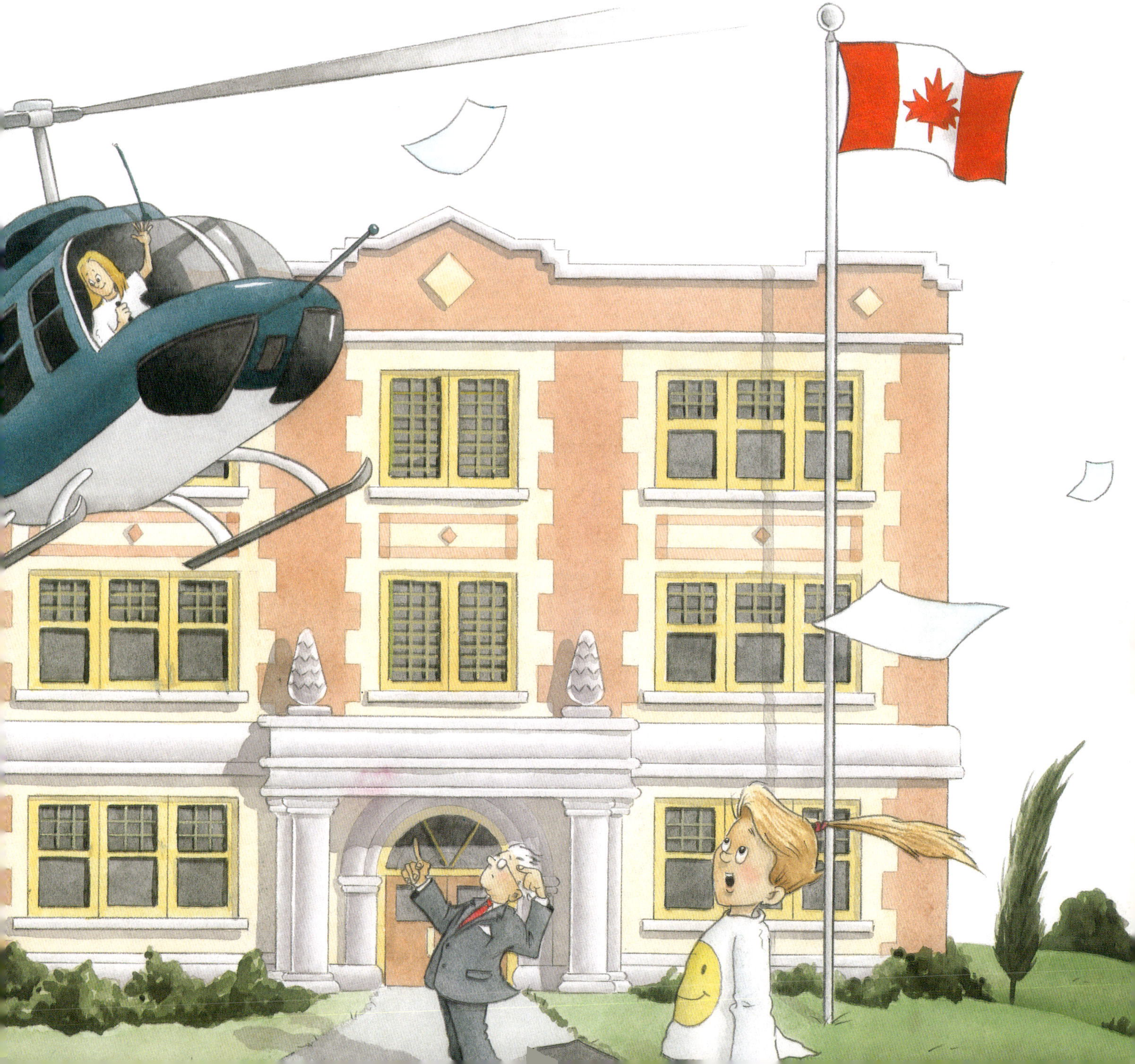

A moment later, I saw something moving on the roof of the school. It was Jenny waving to me.

The principal was yelling up at her. "Jenny, get down here at once!"

"She's not Jenny," I said. "She's a helicopter pilot. That's how she got on the roof."

"I am *not* a helicopter pilot," Jenny called down. "I am a famous scientist and I'm working on an important experiment."

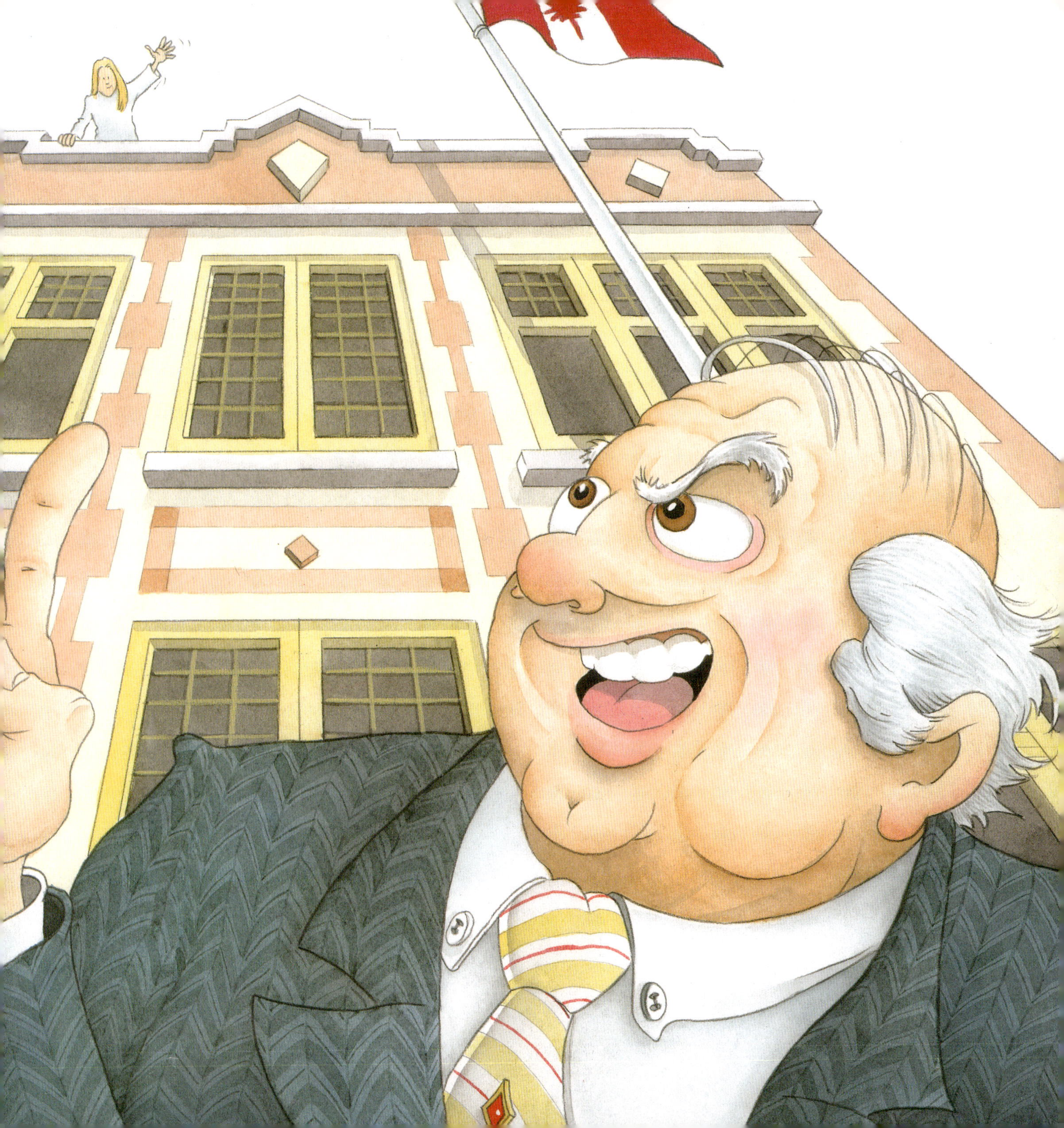

The principal scratched his head.

Instantly, a set of test tubes filled with bubbling chemicals appeared on a table beside Jenny.

"And now for my famous experiment!" Jenny announced to the crowd below her.

She took a test tube in each hand. She poured the liquid from one test tube into the liquid of the other.

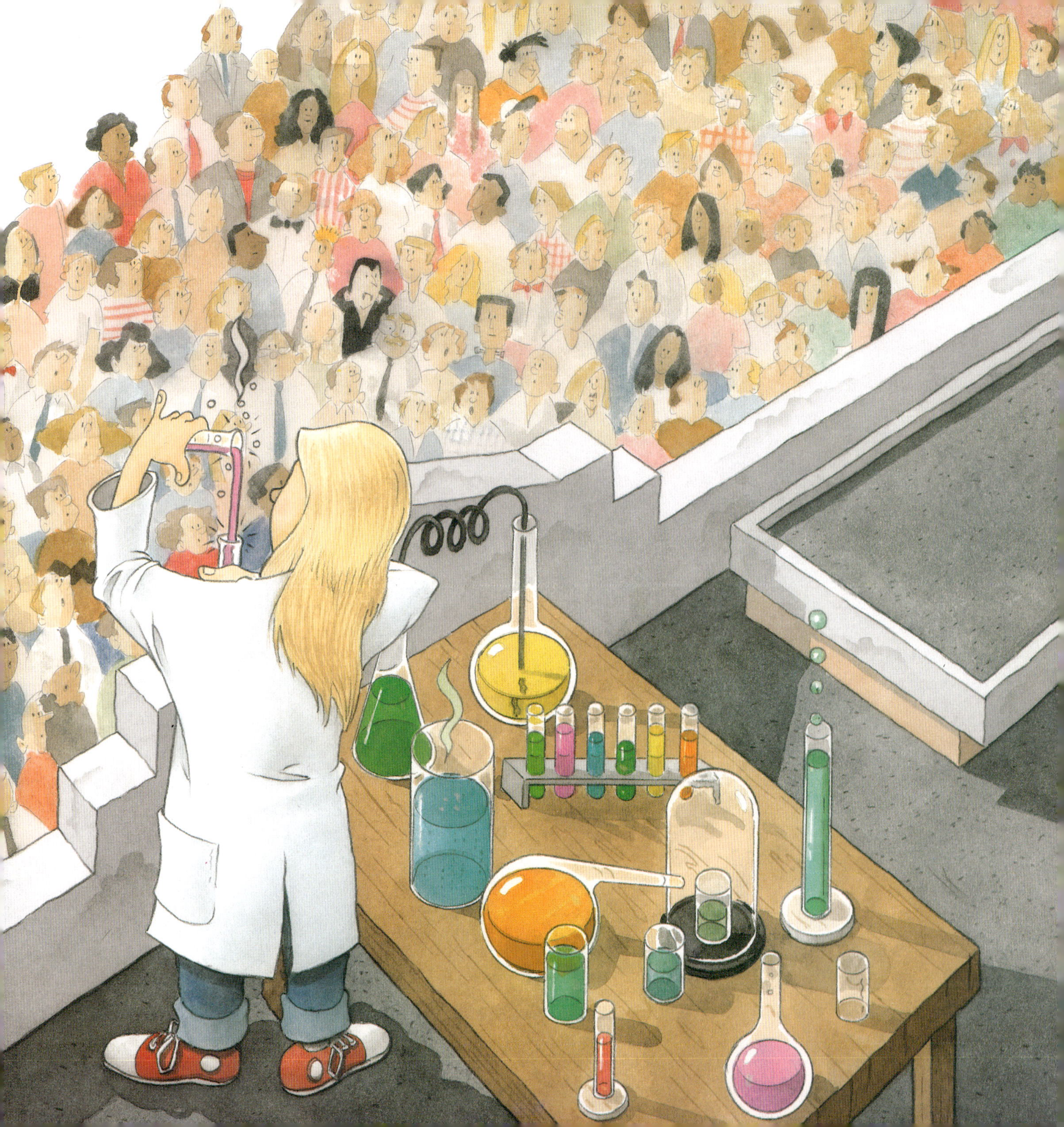

BOOM!

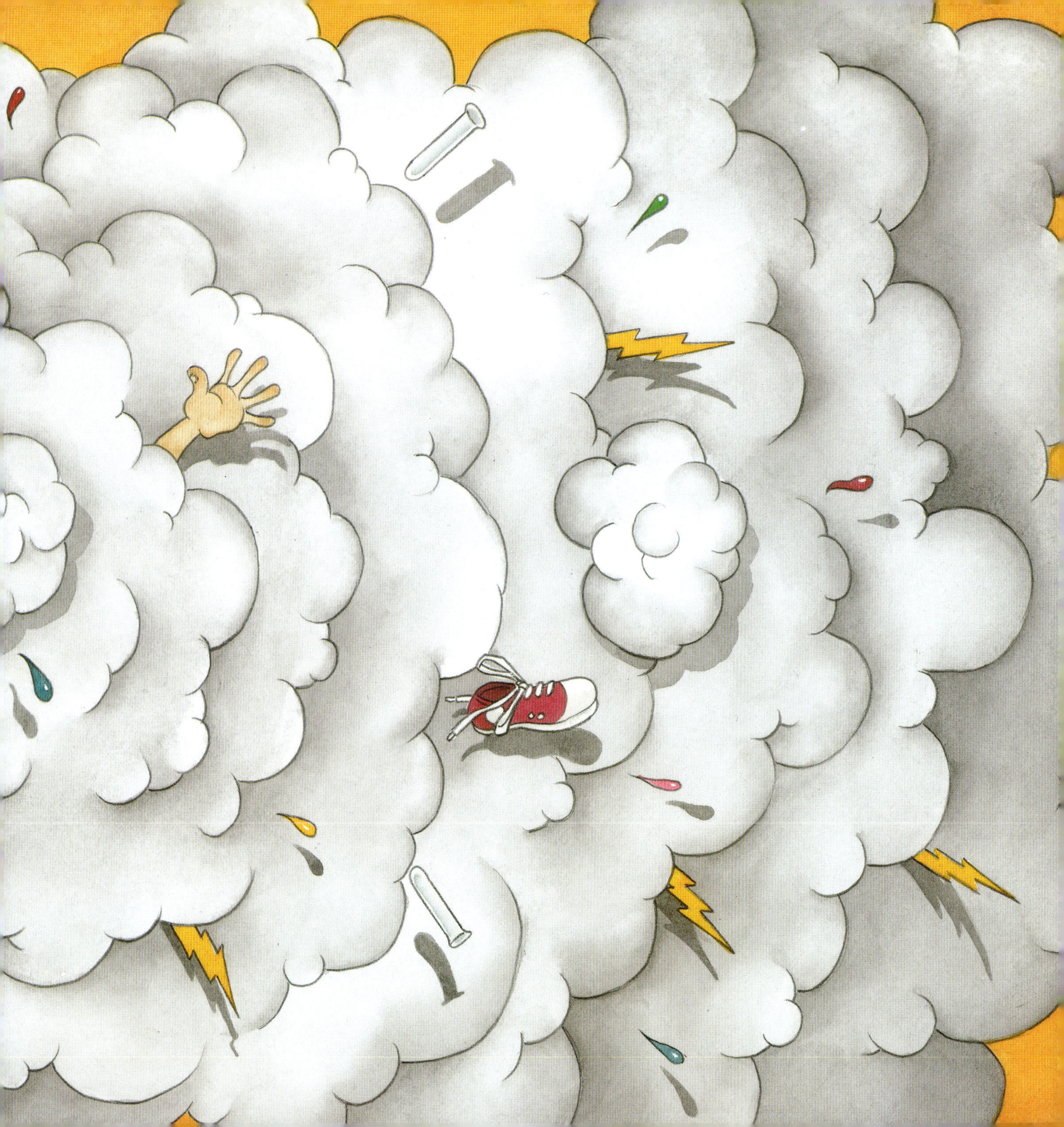

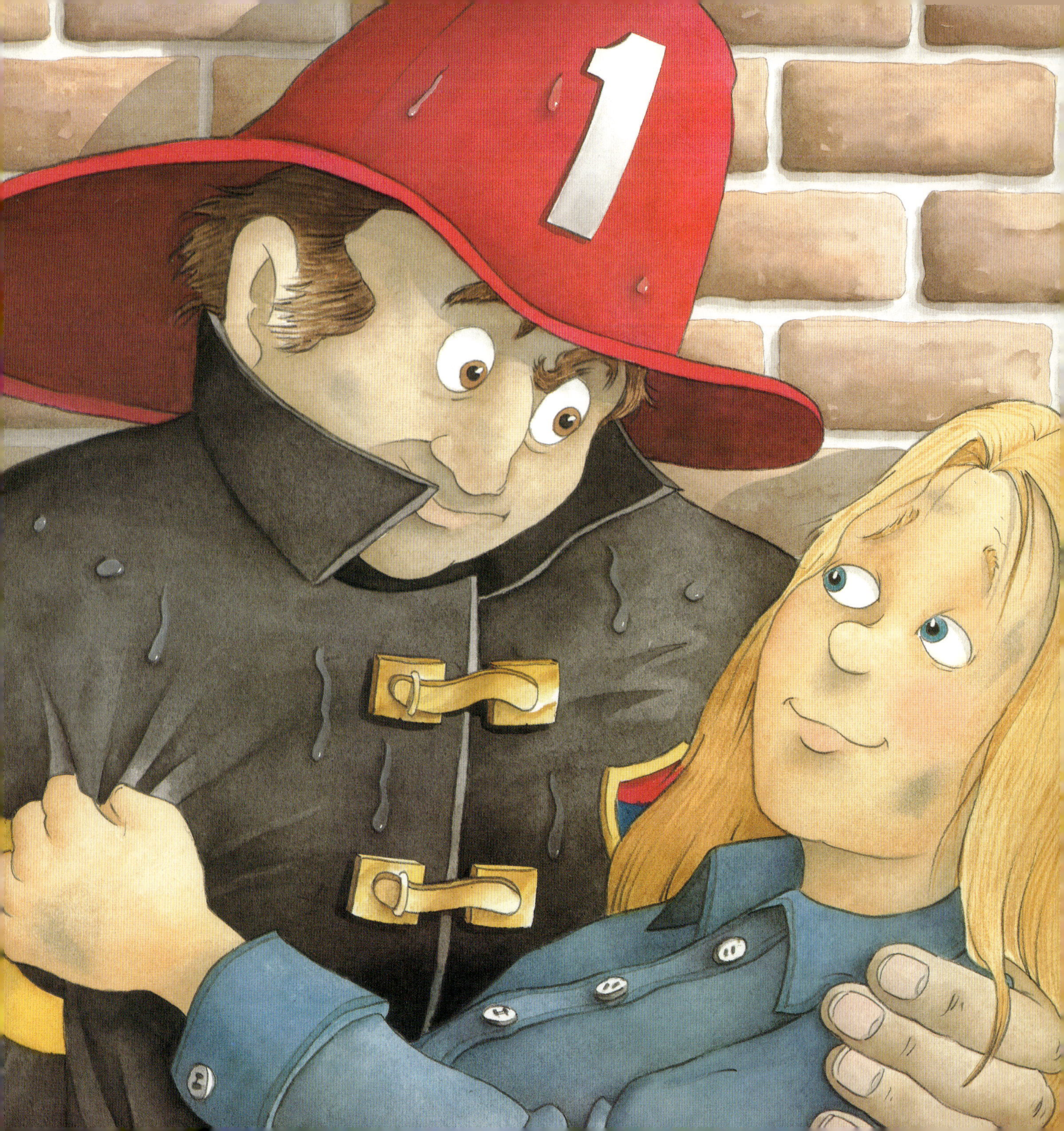

The table went up in flames. Jenny screamed, "Help!"

The school alarm went off. A fire engine roared up with its siren wailing. A firefighter clambered up a ladder onto the roof. A moment later, he carried Jenny down to the playground. Water from the thick hoses put the fire out.

The firefighter who had rescued Jenny asked, "Are you hurt? What were you doing up on the roof? How did the fire get started?"

"Well," I said, "you see, Jenny is a famous scientist and she was doing this experiment when —"

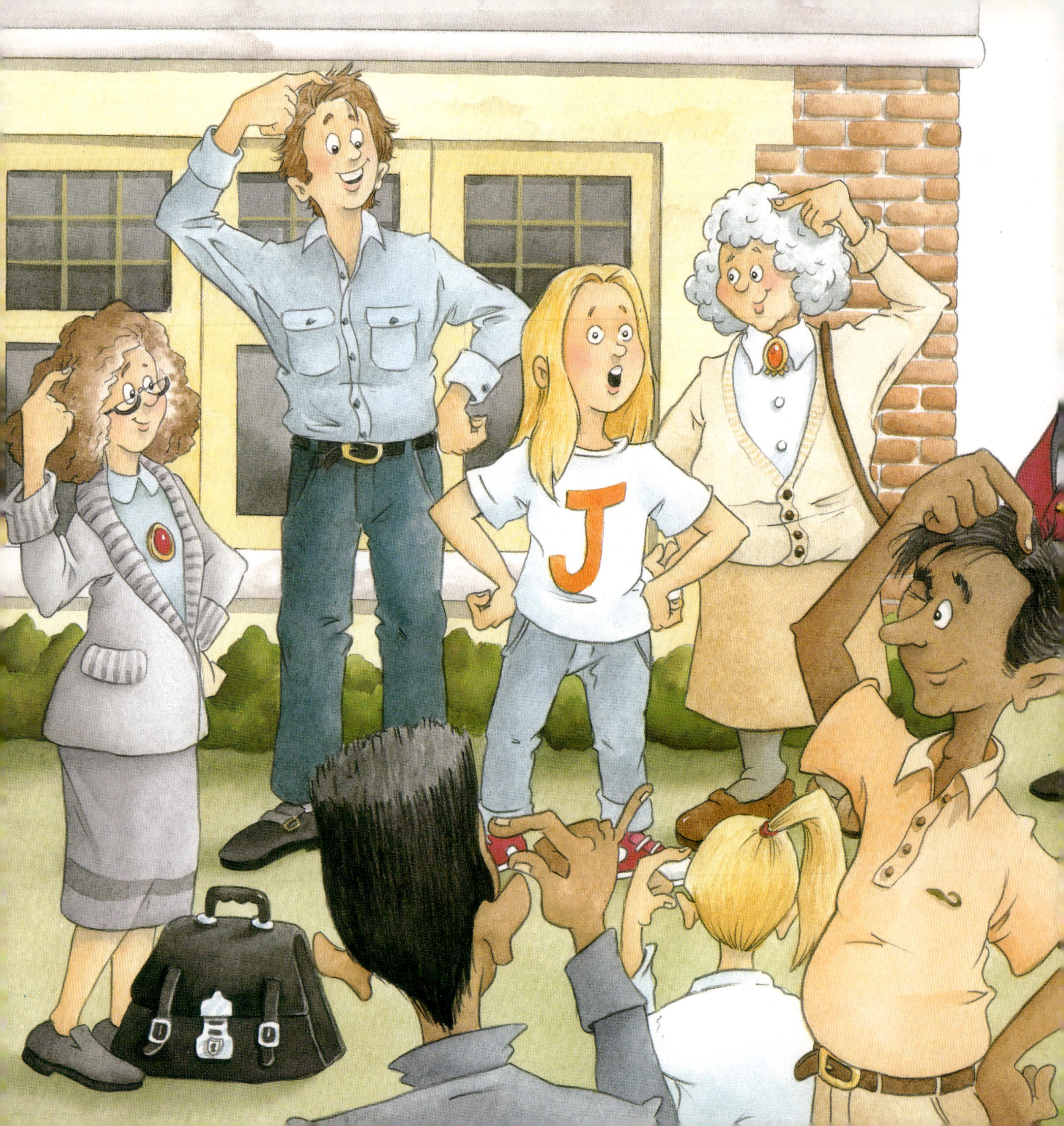
J

"I am *not* a famous scientist," Jenny interrupted. "I am a girl, and my name is Jenny."

We quickly scratched our heads.

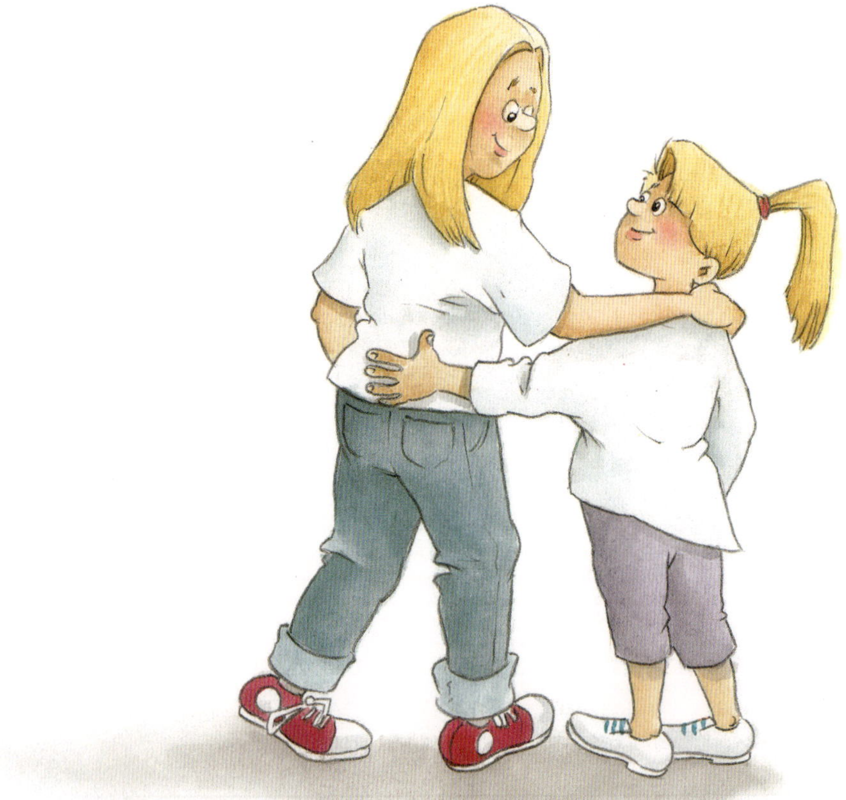